Easy Parsnip Cookbook

50 Delicious Parsnip Recipes; Techniques
for Cooking with Parsnips

By
BookSumo Press

Published by
http://www.booksumo.com

Table of Contents

Mashed Potato Alternative II

Prep Time: 10 mins
Total Time: 40 mins

Servings per Recipe: 8
Calories   143 kcal
Fat   10.7 g
Carbohydrates   7.1g
Protein   5 g
Cholesterol   31 mg
Sodium   441 mg

Ingredients

5 C. whole milk
10 parsnips, peeled and cubed
1 tsp salt
1/4 C. butter
1 tsp dried thyme

1/2 tsp ground black pepper
salt or to taste

Directions

1. In a large pan, heat the milk on medium heat till warmed and just under a boil.
2. Stir in the parsnips and 1 tsp of the salt and cook, covered for about 25-30 minutes.
3. Drain the parsnips, reserving the warm milk in a bowl.
4. In the same pan, add the parsnips, 1 C. of the reserved warm milk, butter, thyme and pepper and with a hand mixer, blend till smooth.
5. Add more milk, salt or pepper as desired.

MASHED POTATO
Alternative of Parsnips with Carrots I

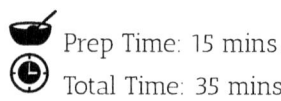

Prep Time: 15 mins
Total Time: 35 mins

Servings per Recipe: 4
Calories	164 kcal
Fat	17.4 g
Carbohydrates	2.7g
Protein	< 0.5 g
Cholesterol	46 mg
Sodium	220 mg

Ingredients

8 parsnips, peeled and cut into 2 inch pieces
2 carrots, peeled and cut into 2-inch pieces
1/4 C. snipped chives

6 tbsp butter, divided
sea salt and freshly ground black pepper to taste

Directions

1. In large pan, place the parsnips, carrots and enough salted water to cover the vegetables.
2. Bring to a boil over high heat.
3. Reduce the heat to medium-low and simmer, covered for about 15-20 minutes.
4. Drain well and return vegetables to pan on low heat.
5. Stir in the chives and 3 tbsp of the butter.
6. With an immersion blender, puree the mixture.
7. Add 3 tbsp of the butter and blend till mixture becomes smooth.
8. Season with the salt and pepper to taste.

Parsnip
Burgers

🍲 Prep Time: 15 mins
🕐 Total Time: 45 mins

Servings per Recipe: 8
Calories	167 kcal
Fat	9.5 g
Carbohydrates	18.4g
Protein	2.9 g
Cholesterol	10 mg
Sodium	137 mg

Ingredients

1 lb. parsnips, peeled and chopped
2 tbsp butter
1/2 small onion, finely chopped
2 tbsp all-purpose flour
1 C. milk

1/2 C. bread crumbs
salt and ground black pepper to taste
2 C. vegetable oil for frying

Directions

1. In large pan, place the parsnips and enough water to cover and bring to a boil.
2. Cook for about 10 minutes.
3. Drain the parsnips and with a potato masher, mash them.
4. Transfer into a bowl and keep aside.
5. In a pan, melt the butter on medium heat.
6. Stir in the onions and cook for about 5 minutes.
7. Add the flour, beating continuously till the mixture becomes paste-like.
8. Slowly, add the milk into the flour mixture, beating continuously and bring to a simmer over medium heat.
9. Cook, stirring continuously for about 10 minutes.
10. Transfer the sauce in the bowl of the mashed parsnips.
11. Add the bread crumbs, salt and pepper and mix well.
12. Make equal sized patties rom the mixture.
13. In a large, deep skillet, heat the oil to 350 degrees F and fry the patties or about 5 minutes, turning once.
14. Transfer the patties onto a paper towel lined plate to drain.
15. Serve hot.

JAPANESE
Teriyaki Parsnips

Prep Time: 5 mins
Total Time: 30 mins

Servings per Recipe: 4

Calories	143 kcal
Fat	3.2 g
Carbohydrates	28.1g
Protein	1.9 g
Cholesterol	8 mg
Sodium	377 mg

Ingredients

1 lb. parsnips, peeled
1 tbsp butter
2 tbsp white sugar

2 tbsp teriyaki sauce

Directions

1. In large pan, place the parsnips and enough water to cover and bring to a boil over high heat.
2. Reduce the heat to medium-low and simmer for about 15 minutes.
3. Drain well and keep aside to cool slightly.
4. Cut the parsnips into 2 1/2-inch sticks.
5. In a skillet, melt the butter on medium heat.
6. Stir in the sugar and parsnips and toss to coat.
7. Add the teriyaki sauce and cook for about 5 minutes.

Potato Chip
Alternative with Parsnips

Prep Time: 30 mins
Total Time: 1 hr

Servings per Recipe: 4
Calories	362 kcal
Fat	23.1 g
Carbohydrates	37.3g
Protein	3.4 g
Cholesterol	31 mg
Sodium	243 mg

Ingredients

4 parsnips
1/4 C. butter, melted
1/2 C. all-purpose flour
2 C. vegetable oil for frying
salt

chili powder
cayenne pepper

Directions

1. Peel the parsnips and slice into 1/4-inch rounds.
2. In a pan of lightly salted boiling water, add parsnips and cook for about 5 minutes.
3. Drain and keep aside to cool slightly.
4. Coat the parsnip slices in the melted butter and arrange onto a baking sheet.
5. Refrigerate for about 30 minutes.
6. Remove from the refrigerator and coat parsnip slices in flour.
7. In a large heavy skillet, heat the oil on medium-high heat and fry the parsnip slices till golden brown from both sides.
8. Transfer the slices onto a paper towel lined plate to drain.
9. Sprinkle with the salt, chili powder and cayenne and serve.

HUNGRY BEE
Parsnips

Prep Time: 10 mins
Total Time: 40 mins

Servings per Recipe: 6
Calories	190 kcal
Fat	2.3 g
Carbohydrates	44.3g
Protein	1.5 g
Cholesterol	5 mg
Sodium	27 mg

Ingredients

1/2 C. warm water
1/2 C. honey
1 tbsp melted butter

5 parsnips, peeled and cubed

Directions

1. Set your oven to 375 degrees F before doing anything else.
2. In a large bowl, add the water, butter, and honey and mix till the honey is dissolved.
3. Add the parsnips and toss to coat.
4. Transfer the parsnips mixture into a 12x9-inch glass baking dish
5. Cook in the oven for about 30 minutes.

Rustic
Oak Wood Soup

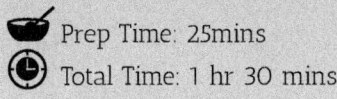 Prep Time: 25mins

Total Time: 1 hr 30 mins

Servings per Recipe: 10

Calories	187 kcal
Fat	9.7 g
Carbohydrates	23.9g
Protein	2.9 g
Cholesterol	22 mg
Sodium	361 mg

Ingredients

2 lb. parsnips, peeled and cut into 1/2 inch pieces
3 carrots, peeled and cut into 1/2-inch pieces
1 tbsp olive oil
sea salt and ground black pepper to taste
1 tbsp olive oil
1 large onion, diced
3 stalks celery, diced
1 tbsp butter
3 cloves garlic, minced

1 tbsp brown sugar
1 tsp ground ginger
1/2 tsp ground cardamom
1/2 tsp ground allspice
1/2 tsp ground cloves
1/4 tsp cayenne pepper
4 C. chicken stock
1 C. whole milk
1/2 C. heavy cream

Directions

1. Set your oven to 425 degrees F before doing anything else.
2. In a bowl, pace the parsnips, carrots, 1 tbsp the olive oil, salt and pepper and toss to coat.
3. Place the vegetables onto baking sheet evenly.
4. Cook in the oven for about 30 minutes.
5. In a large pan, heat the remaining 1 tbsp of the olive oil on medium heat and sauté the onion and celery for about 7 minutes.
6. Reduce the heat to low and stir in the butter, garlic, brown sugar and the roasted parsnips and carrots and cook for about 10 minutes.
7. Stir in the ginger, cardamom, allspice, cloves and cayenne pepper and cook for about 1 minute.
8. Add the chicken stock and bring to a boil on medium-high heat.
9. Reduce the heat to medium-low and simmer, partially covered for about 15 minutes.
10. Remove from the heat and keep aside to cool slightly.

11. In a blender, add the soup in batches and pulse till smooth.
12. Return the soup into a pan on medium-low heat.
13. Stir in the milk, cream, salt and pepper before serving.

How to
Cook Parsnips

Prep Time: 10 mins
Total Time: 40 mins

Servings per Recipe: 4

Calories	111 kcal
Fat	3.2 g
Carbohydrates	20.6g
Protein	1.4 g
Cholesterol	8 mg
Sodium	32 mg

Ingredients

1 lb. parsnips, peeled, cut in half crosswise, and cut into narrow strips lengthwise
1 tbsp butter

1 pinch salt
ground black pepper to taste

Directions

1. In large pan, place the parsnips and enough water to cover and bring to a boil over high heat.
2. Reduce the heat and simmer for about 15-20 minutes.
3. Drain well and pat dry with a paper towel.
4. Keep aside to cool slightly.
5. In a skillet, melt the butter on medium heat.
6. Arrange the parsnips into the hot butter in an even layer.
7. Sprinkle the parsnips with the salt and black pepper and cook for about 5-8 minutes per side.

NEW ENGLAND STYLE
Chowder

Prep Time: 20 mins
Total Time: 50 mins

Servings per Recipe: 7

Calories	348 kcal
Fat	19.2 g
Carbohydrates	22.2g
Protein	22.8 g
Cholesterol	101 mg
Sodium	437 mg

Ingredients

1 lb. cod fillets
1/2 lb. lightly smoked cod, skin and bones removed
1/2 lemon
1 sprig fresh thyme
1 lb. parsnip, chopped
1/2 lb. potatoes

3 tbsp butter
1 onion, chopped
1 C. milk
1 C. heavy whipping cream
salt to taste
ground black pepper to taste

Directions

1. If the smoked cod has a strong smoky flavor, soak it in water for about 30 minutes.
2. Drain well and rinse.
3. In a large pan, add the cod, smoked cod, 1 tbsp. of lemon juice, thyme and enough water to cover and bring to a gentle simmer. Poach the fish for about 8-10 minutes.
4. Transfer the fish into a bowl, reserving the poaching liquid. Keep aside the fish to cool.
5. Now, break the cod it into large bite-sized pieces and keep aside.
6. Meanwhile peel the parsnips and cut into 1/4-inch thick slices.
7. Peel the potatoes and cut into 1/2-inch cubes.
8. In a bowl of water, place the potatoes to prevent discoloring.
9. In a large pan, melt 2 tbsp of the butter on medium heat and sauté the onion till golden.
10. Add the parsnips, potatoes and 3 C. of the reserved poaching liquid and bring to a boil.
11. Reduce the heat and simmer, covered for about 15 minutes.
12. In a small pan, heat the milk and cream but do not boil.
13. Add the milk mixture into the vegetable mixture and stir to combine.
14. Stir in the cod, smoked cod, salt and freshly ground pepper.
15. Just before serving stir in the remaining butter. Serve with a topping of the chives.

November's
Veggies

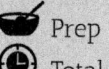 Prep Time: 20 mins

Total Time: 35 mins

Servings per Recipe: 8

Calories	163 kcal
Fat	6.3 g
Carbohydrates	26.7g
Protein	2 g
Cholesterol	15 mg
Sodium	190 mg

Ingredients

1/4 C. butter
4 large carrots, cut into 3-inch x 1/2-inch pieces
4 large parsnips, cut into 3-inch x 1/2-inch pieces
3/4 C. orange juice
3/4 C. chicken stock

2 tbsp lemon juice
salt and ground black pepper to taste
3 tbsp chopped fresh chives

Directions

1. In a large skillet, melt the butter on medium heat and stir fry the carrots and parsnips for about 8-10 minutes.
2. Stir in the orange juice, chicken stock, lemon juice, salt and black pepper and bring to a boil.
3. Reduce the heat to low and simmer, covered for about 10 minutes, stirring occasionally.
4. Season with more salt and black pepper if required.
5. Serve with a topping of the chives.

BALSAMIC PARSNIPS
and Brussel Sprouts

Prep Time: 15 mins
Total Time: 55 mins

Servings per Recipe: 4

Calories	222 kcal
Fat	6.7 g
Carbohydrates	39.6g
Protein	5.6 g
Cholesterol	0 mg
Sodium	276 mg

Ingredients

1/3 C. balsamic vinaigrette salad
dressing (such as Kraft(R))
1 tbsp brown sugar
1 tbsp chopped fresh thyme
1 lb. Brussels sprouts, halved

1 lb. parsnips, peeled
1 large red onion, thickly sliced

Directions

1. Set your oven to 400 degrees F before doing anything else.
2. In a bowl, mix together the salad dressing, brown sugar and thyme.
3. In a 13x9-inch baking dish, add the Brussels sprouts, parsnips, red onion and dressing mixture and toss to coat.
4. Cook in the oven for about 40 minutes.

Whipping
the Parsnips

🍜 Prep Time: 15 mins
🕐 Total Time: 1 hr

Servings per Recipe: 6
Calories   404 kcal
Fat   23.8 g
Carbohydrates   46.6 g
Protein   3.7 g
Cholesterol   64 mg
Sodium   643 mg

Ingredients

3 lb. parsnips, peeled and cut into 1/2-inch pieces
1/4 lb. butter, melted
1/4 C. sherry
1/4 C. heavy whipping cream

1 tsp salt
1 tsp white sugar
1/4 C. bread crumbs
2 tbsp butter, cut into small pieces

Directions

1. In a large pan, add the parsnips and enough water to cover and bring to a boil.
2. Reduce heat to medium-low and simmer for about 20-30 minutes.
3. Drain well and keep aside to cool slightly.
4. Set your oven to 350 degrees F.
5. In a bowl, add the parsnips, melted butter, sherry, heavy whipping cream, salt and white sugar and beat till smooth.
6. Place the mixture into a baking dish and top with the bread crumbs evenly.
7. Place the butter on top in the form of dots.
8. Cook in the oven for about 25-30 minutes.

FRIGID
Winter Soup

Prep Time: 35 mins
Total Time: 55 mins

Servings per Recipe: 30
Calories	92 kcal
Fat	5.3 g
Carbohydrates	9.7g
Protein	1.5 g
Cholesterol	2 mg
Sodium	< 344 mg

Ingredients

1/3 C. extra-virgin olive oil
2 large carrots, peeled and chopped
2 celery ribs, chopped
1 white onion, peeled and chopped
3 large Portobello mushroom caps, cleaned and chopped
5 (13.75 oz.) cans chicken broth
8 parsnips, peeled and chopped

2 C. fresh shiitake mushrooms, sliced
1/3 C. extra-virgin olive oil
5 cloves garlic, minced
1 bunch fresh tarragon
3 sprigs fresh thyme
kosher salt to taste (optional)

Directions

1. In a deep pan, heat 1/3 C. of the olive oil on medium heat and sauté the carrots, celery, and onion for about 5 minutes.
2. Stir in the Portobello mushrooms and cook for about 5 minutes.
3. Add the chicken broth, parsnips and shiitake mushrooms and bring to a boil.
4. Reduce the heat to medium and simmer for about 10 minutes.
5. Remove from the heat.
6. In a blender, place 1/3 C. of the olive oil, garlic, tarragon and thyme and pulse till well combined.
7. Stir the mixture into the soup with the kosher salt.

Tuesday's
Pancakes

Prep Time: 10 mins
Total Time: 25 mins

Servings per Recipe: 2

Calories	194 kcal
Fat	13 g
Carbohydrates	14.7g
Protein	5.8 g
Cholesterol	138 mg
Sodium	641 mg

Ingredients

1 C. grated peeled parsnips
2 small eggs
1/4 C. finely chopped onion
1 tbsp olive oil
1/2 tsp salt

1/2 tsp dried rosemary
ground black pepper to taste (optional)
1 tsp sunflower oil

Directions

1. In a bowl, add the parsnips, eggs, onion, olive oil, salt, rosemary and black pepper and mix till well combined and lumpy.
2. In a heavy frying pan, heat the sunflower oil on medium heat.
3. With a spoon, place the mixture into the oil and fry for about 6 - 7 minutes per side.

APPLE
Dijon Veggie Roast

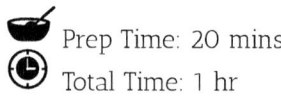 Prep Time: 20 mins

Total Time: 1 hr

Servings per Recipe: 8

Calories	161 kcal
Fat	4.1 g
Carbohydrates	31.2g
Protein	2 g
Cholesterol	0 mg
Sodium	211 mg

Ingredients

2/3 C. apple cider
2 tbsp olive oil
2 tbsp apple cider vinegar
2 tbsp coarse-grain Dijon mustard
2 tbsp honey
2 tsp chopped fresh thyme
1/4 tsp salt

1 1/2 lb. carrots, peeled and cut into sticks
1 1/2 lb. parsnips, peeled and cut into sticks
Aluminum foil

Directions

1. Set your oven to 400 degrees F before doing anything else and line a roasting pan with a piece of foil.
2. In a very large bowl, add the apple cider, oil, vinegar, mustard, honey, thyme and salt and beat till well combined.
3. Add the carrots and parsnips and toss to coat.
4. Place the vegetables mixture onto the prepared roasting pan in an even layer.
5. Cook in the oven for about 35 minutes, stirring twice.

A Country
Dinner

Prep Time: 15 mins
Total Time: 1 hr

Servings per Recipe: 6

Calories	212 kcal
Fat	16 g
Carbohydrates	12.9 g
Protein	6.2 g
Cholesterol	55 mg
Sodium	332 mg

Ingredients

3 Yukon Gold potatoes, peeled
2 parsnips, peeled
2 cloves garlic, minced
1 tbsp butter, melted
salt and ground black pepper to taste
1 tsp fresh thyme leaves, divided
2 oz. finely grated Parmigiano-Reggiano

cheese, divided
3/4 C. crème fraiche, divided
1 C. chicken broth
1 pinch cayenne pepper

Directions

1. Set your oven to 375 degrees F before doing anything else.
2. In a large bowl, of cold water, place the potatoes and parsnips.
3. In a large baking dish, spread the garlic and melted butter evenly.
4. With a mandolin slicer, slice the potatoes very thinly.
5. With a vegetable peeler, slice the parsnips thinly.
6. In the bottom of the prepared baking dish, place 1/3 of the potato slices and sprinkle with the salt and black pepper, followed by a few thyme leaves and a light dusting of Parmigiano-Reggiano cheese. Top with about 3 tbsp of the crème fraiche.
7. Arrange 1/2 of the parsnip slices over the crème fraiche in an even layer and sprinkle with the salt and black pepper.
8. Repeat the layering process as 1/3 potato slices, salt, black pepper, thyme, Parmigiano-Reggiano cheese, crème fraiche, and remaining 1/2 parsnip slices. Sprinkle with the salt.
9. Top with remaining 1/3 of the potato slices and sprinkle with the salt.
10. Slowly, place the chicken broth, about 3 tbsp at a time. Shake the dish gently to eliminate air bubbles. Gently spread the remaining 2 tbsp crème fraiche over the potatoes.
11. Sprinkle cayenne and remaining Parmigiano-Reggiano cheese over the top.
12. Cook in the oven for about 45-60 minutes.

PARSNIP
Possibilities

Prep Time: 15 mins
Total Time: 30 mins

Servings per Recipe: 8
Calories	222 kcal
Fat	12.1 g
Carbohydrates	28.6g
Protein	2.3 g
Cholesterol	31 mg
Sodium	152 mg

Ingredients

1 1/2 lb. carrots, coarsely chopped
2 lb. parsnips, peeled and cut into 1 1/2 inch pieces
1/2 C. butter, diced
1 pinch ground cloves

salt to taste
ground black pepper to taste

Directions

1. In large pan of the salted boiling water, add the carrots and simmer partially, covered for about 5 minutes.
2. Add the parsnips and simmer partially, covered for about 15 minutes.
3. Drain well.
4. Return vegetables to the pan on medium heat and stir till any excess moisture evaporates.
5. In a food processor, add the vegetables, butter and pulse till smooth.
6. Season with the cloves, salt and pepper.
7. Transfer into a bowl and serve.

Aromatic
Garlic and Honey Parsnips

Prep Time: 15 mins
Total Time: 45 mins

Servings per Recipe: 4
Calories	154 kcal
Fat	3.8 g
Carbohydrates	30.3g
Protein	1.9 g
Cholesterol	0 mg
Sodium	375 mg

Ingredients

4 parsnips, peeled and cut into large sticks
1 tbsp olive oil
2 cloves garlic, minced
1 tbsp honey
3/4 tsp kosher salt

ground black pepper, to taste
1 tbsp chopped fresh mint
1 tbsp chopped fresh sage

Directions

1. Set your oven to 450 degrees F before doing anything else.
2. In a large bowl, add the parsnips, olive oil, garlic, honey, salt and black pepper and toss to coat well.
3. Spread the parsnip mixture onto a baking sheet. In an even layer.
4. Cook in the oven for about 30 minutes.
5. Transfer into a bowl and toss with the mint and sage.

TRALEE
Side Dish

Prep Time: 15 mins
Total Time: 40 mins

Servings per Recipe: 6

Calories	354 kcal
Fat	23.4 g
Carbohydrates	36.2g
Protein	3.3 g
Cholesterol	68 mg
Sodium	266 mg

Ingredients

6 carrots, peeled and chopped
4 large parsnips, peeled and chopped
2 turnips, peeled and chopped
1/2 C. butter
1/2 C. heavy whipping cream

1/4 tsp ground cloves
1 pinch cayenne pepper
salt and ground black pepper to taste

Directions

1. In a large pan, add the carrots, parsnips, turnips and enough lightly salted cold water to cover and bring to a boil.
2. Cook for about 25 minutes.
3. Drain the vegetables and return to the pan.
4. Add the butter, cream, cloves, cayenne pepper, salt, and black pepper and with a potato masher, mash roughly.

Wendy's
Root Vegetable Casseroles

Prep Time: 15 mins
Total Time: 1 hr 30 mins

Servings per Recipe: 8
Calories	407 kcal
Fat	18.2 g
Carbohydrates	55.1g
Protein	9 g
Cholesterol	49 mg
Sodium	258 mg

Ingredients

7 C. low-sodium chicken broth
3 lb. baking potatoes, peeled and cubed
1 1/2 lb. rutabagas, peeled and cubed
1 1/4 lb. parsnips, peeled and cubed
8 cloves garlic
1 bay leaf

1 tsp dried thyme
3/4 C. butter, softened
3 onions, thinly sliced
salt and ground black pepper to taste

Directions

1. In a large pan, mix together the chicken broth, potatoes, rutabagas, parsnips, garlic, bay leaf and thyme and bring to a boil.
2. Reduce the heat and simmer partially, covered for about 30 minutes.
3. Drain the vegetables and transfer into a large bowl.
4. Add 1/2 C. of the butter, salt and pepper and with an electric mixer, beat till mashed but still chunky.
5. Set your oven to 375 degrees F.
6. Transfer the mashed vegetables into a greased 13x9x2-inch baking dish.
7. In a heavy large skillet, melt the remaining 1/4 C. of the butter on medium-high heat and sauté the onions for about 5 minutes.
8. Reduce the heat to medium-low and sauté the onions for about 15 minutes.
9. Season with the salt and pepper.
10. Spread the onions evenly over mashed vegetables evenly.
11. Cook in the oven for about 25 minutes.

5-INGREDIENT
Parsnips

Prep Time: 10 mins
Total Time: 50 mins

Servings per Recipe: 4
Calories	225 kcal
Fat	7.2 g
Carbohydrates	41.5g
Protein	1.8 g
Cholesterol	0 mg
Sodium	49 mg

Ingredients

3 carrots, peeled
3 parsnips, peeled
2 tbsp olive oil

1/4 C. honey
salt and ground black pepper to taste

Directions

1. Set your oven to 350 degrees F before doing anything else.
2. In a bowl, add all the
3. Ingredients and toss to coat.
4. In a baking dish, arrange the vegetable mixture.
5. Cook in the oven for about 40 minutes.

Sweet Potato
and Parsnip Festival

Prep Time: 20 mins
Total Time: 1 hr 5 mins

Servings per Recipe: 4
Calories	218 kcal
Fat	7 g
Carbohydrates	37.7g
Protein	2.4 g
Cholesterol	0 mg
Sodium	79 mg

Ingredients

1 lb. sweet potatoes, cut into long, thin rectangles
1 large carrot, cut into long, thin rectangles
1 parsnip, cut into long, thin rectangles
extra-virgin olive oil, or as needed
salt and ground black pepper to taste

4 sprigs fresh thyme
2 tbsp maple syrup

Directions

1. Set your oven to 375 degrees F before doing anything else.
2. In a jelly roll pan, spread the sweet potato, carrot and parsnip in an even layer.
3. Drizzle with the olive oil and sprinkle with the salt and black pepper.
4. Cook in the oven for about 30 minutes.
5. Place the thyme sprigs over vegetables and drizzle with the maple syrup.
6. Cook in the oven for about 15 minutes more.

FALL-TIME
Casserole

Prep Time: 20 mins
Total Time: 1 hr 15 mins

Servings per Recipe: 8

Calories	438 kcal
Fat	18.4 g
Carbohydrates	57.2g
Protein	14.3 g
Cholesterol	53 mg
Sodium	513 mg

Ingredients

3 C. milk
3 carrots, peeled and diced
2 sweet potatoes, peeled and diced
2 leeks, finely chopped (white part only)
2 parsnips, peeled and diced
2 stalks celery, diced
1 butternut squash, peeled and diced
1 small turnip, peeled and diced

1 (8 oz.) package cream cheese, cubed
1 C. shredded Parmesan cheese
1 pinch ground cloves
salt and ground black pepper to taste
1 C. fine bread crumbs
2 tbsp melted butter

Directions

1. Set your oven to 350 degrees F before doing anything else and grease a casserole dish.
2. In a large pan, add the milk, carrots, sweet potatoes, leeks, parsnips, celery, butternut squash and turnip and bring to a boil.
3. Reduce the heat to medium low and simmer for about 15 minutes, stirring occasionally.
4. Add the cream cheese and stir till melted completely.
5. Stir in the Parmesan cheese, cloves, salt and pepper.
6. Transfer the mixture into the prepared casserole dish.
7. In a bowl, mix together the bread crumbs and melted butter.
8. Spread the crumb mixture over casserole evenly.
9. Cover the casserole dish and cook in the oven for about 30 minutes.
10. Uncover and cook in the oven for about 5 minutes more.

Sunday's
Dinner Pie

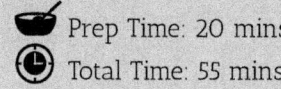 Prep Time: 20 mins

Total Time: 55 mins

Servings per Recipe: 6

Calories	301 kcal
Fat	13.6 g
Carbohydrates	39.6g
Protein	6.2 g
Cholesterol	18 mg
Sodium	869 mg

Ingredients

3 parsnips, peeled and cut into 1/2 inch pieces
3 carrots, peeled and cut into 1/2 inch pieces
1 sweet potato, peeled and cut into 1/2 inch pieces
3 tbsp butter
2 C. sliced mushrooms
1 C. chopped leeks

3 tbsp all-purpose flour
2 C. vegetable broth
1/8 tsp dried thyme
salt and ground black pepper to taste
1/4 tsp hot pepper sauce
2 1/4 C. biscuit baking mix
3/4 C. milk

Directions

1. Set your oven to 400 degrees F before doing anything else.
2. In large pan, place the parsnips, carrots, sweet potato and enough salted water to cover the vegetables. Bring to a boil over high heat.
3. Reduce the heat to medium-low and simmer, covered for about 10 minutes.
4. Drain well and keep aside for about 1-2 minutes.
5. In a large skillet, melt the butter on medium heat and cook the mushrooms and leeks for about 5 minutes. Slowly, add the flour, beating continuously and cook for about 5 minutes.
6. Slowly, add the vegetable broth, beating continuously.
7. Stir in the thyme, salt, pepper and hot pepper sauce.
8. Then, stir in the drained vegetables.
9. Transfer the vegetable mixture into a 10-inch deep pie dish.
10. For biscuit topping in a bowl, mix together the biscuit mix and milk.
11. Place heaping tbsp of the mixture onto vegetable filling. (Do not cover filling completely)
12. Cook in the oven for about 18-20 minutes.

ROOT VEGETABLE
Combo

Prep Time: 10 mins
Total Time: 55 mins

Servings per Recipe: 14
Calories	135 kcal
Fat	2.6 g
Carbohydrates	27.4g
Protein	2.8 g
Cholesterol	0 mg
Sodium	116 mg

Ingredients

parsnips, peeled
6 large carrots, peeled
1 celery root, peeled
1 rutabaga, peeled
1 yellow onion, peeled
3 tbsp minced garlic
3 tbsp dried rosemary

2 tbsp extra-virgin olive oil
sea salt and freshly ground black pepper
to taste

Directions

1. Set your oven to 450 degrees F before doing anything else.
2. Chop the parsnips, carrots, celery root, rutabaga and yellow onion into 1-inch pieces and place in a large sealable container.
3. Add the garlic, rosemary, olive oil, salt and pepper.
4. Seal the container and shake well to coat the vegetables evenly.
5. In two 13x9-inch baking dishes, divide the vegetables in a single layer.
6. Place the remaining oil and seasonings from container over the vegetables.
7. Cook in the oven for about 45 minutes.

Harvest Moon
Mash

🥣 Prep Time: 20 mins
🕐 Total Time: 40 mins

Servings per Recipe: 6
Calories   318 kcal
Fat   8.3 g
Carbohydrates   57.5g
Protein   5.9 g
Cholesterol   20 mg
Sodium   194 mg

Ingredients

1 large yam, peeled and cubed
1 large red potato, peeled and cubed
1 large white potato, peeled and cubed
1 large yellow potato, peeled and cubed
1 large beet, peeled and cubed
1 rutabaga, peeled and cubed (optional)
1 parsnip, peeled and cubed (optional)

1 turnip, peeled and cubed
1/4 C. butter, room temperature
1 pinch ground cloves (optional)
salt and ground black pepper to taste

Directions

1. In a large pan, place the yam, red potato, white potato, yellow potato, beet, rutabaga, parsnip, turnip and enough salted water to cover and bring to a boil.
2. Reduce the heat to medium-low and simmer for about 20-25 minutes.
3. Drain and return to the pan.
4. Add the butter and with a potato masher, mash till smooth.
5. Season with the cloves, salt and black pepper

PICARESQUE
Parsnips

Prep Time: 25 mins
Total Time: 1 hr

Servings per Recipe: 8

Calories	235 kcal
Fat	8.9 g
Carbohydrates	37.4g
Protein	2.9 g
Cholesterol	0 mg
Sodium	718 mg

Ingredients

1 C. cubed red potatoes
1 large yam, peeled and chopped
4 large carrots, peeled and sliced
1 large parsnip, peeled and chopped
1 jicama, peeled and chopped
2 turnips, peeled and chopped
1/4 C. minced fresh rosemary

5 tbsp olive oil
6 cloves garlic, minced
1 tbsp sea salt

Directions

1. Set your oven to 400 degrees F before doing anything else.
2. In a large baking dish, mix together the red potatoes, yam, carrots, parsnip, jicama and turnips.
3. In a small bowl, mix together the rosemary, olive oil, garlic and sea salt.
4. Place the oil mixture over vegetables and toss to coat.
5. Cook in the oven for about 35-45 minutes.

Verdant Bluffs Roast

Prep Time: 40 mins
Total Time: 1 hr 30 mins

Servings per Recipe: 6
Calories	99 kcal
Fat	4.8 g
Carbohydrates	13.8g
Protein	1.3 g
Cholesterol	0 mg
Sodium	67 mg

Ingredients

5 lb. rutabaga, peeled and cut into 2x1/2 inch pieces
5 lb. parsnips, peeled and cut into 2x1/2 inch pieces
5 lb. carrots, peeled and cut into 2x1/2 inch pieces
3/4 tsp salt

1 1/4 C. vegetable oil
1/4 C. dried basil
salt and ground black pepper to taste
1 1/4 C. chopped fresh parsley

Directions

1. In a pan, place the rutabaga, 1/4 tsp of salt and enough water to cover and bring to a boil.
2. Reduce the heat to medium and simmer, covered for about 5 minutes.
3. Drain well and keep aside to cool completely.
4. Repeat the steps to cook the parsnips and carrots.
5. Place the cooled vegetables in the resealable freezer bags.
6. Refrigerate for about 1-2 days or freeze up to 1 month.
7. To thaw the vegetables, refrigerate overnight and drain.
8. Set your oven to 425 degrees F.
9. Place the vegetable oil into a rimmed baking dish.
10. Place the pan in preheated oven to heat for 5 minutes.
11. In a large bowl, add the vegetables, basil, salt and pepper and toss to coat well.
12. Add the vegetables in the heated oven and toss to coat with the oil.
13. Cook in the oven for about 30 minutes, flipping after every 10 minutes.
14. Serve with a sprinkling of the parsley.

VENISON
Vegetable Stew

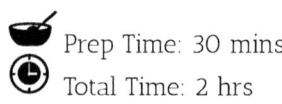 Prep Time: 30 mins
Total Time: 2 hrs

Servings per Recipe: 7

Calories	408 kcal
Fat	7.5 g
Carbohydrates	50g
Protein	35 g
Cholesterol	110 mg
Sodium	1105 mg

Ingredients

2 tbsp vegetable oil
2 lb. venison stew meat
3 onions, chopped
2 cloves garlic, minced
1 tbsp Worcestershire sauce
1 bay leaf
1/2 tsp dried thyme

1 tbsp salt
3 C. water
7 small potatoes, peeled and quartered
1 lb. parsnip, chopped
1/4 C. all-purpose flour
1/4 C. water

Directions

1. In a large soup pan, heat the oil and brown the meat completely.
2. Stir in the onions, garlic. Worcestershire sauce, bay leaf, thyme, salt and 3 C. of the water and simmer, covered for about 1 1/2-2 hours.
3. Stir in the potatoes and parsnips and cook till tender.
4. In a bowl, mix together the flour and 1/4 C. of the water.
5. Stir the flour mixture into the stew.
6. Discard the bay leaf before serving.

Skyhall
Soup

Prep Time: 20 mins
Total Time: 1 hr

Servings per Recipe: 6

Calories	236 kcal
Fat	5.6 g
Carbohydrates	36.9 g
Protein	11.2 g
Cholesterol	0 mg
Sodium	438 mg

Ingredients

2 tbsp olive oil
1 large onion, diced
2 carrots, peeled and sliced
2 parsnips, peeled and sliced
1 golden beet, peeled and diced
1/2 large rutabaga, diced
1 bulb fennel, diced

4 C. vegetable broth
1 C. dried lentils
1/4 tsp dried thyme
2 bay leaves
1 bunch fresh parsley, finely chopped
salt and ground black pepper to taste

Directions

1. In a large pan, heat the oil on medium heat and cook the onion, carrots, parsnips, beet, rutabaga and fennel for about 5 minutes.
2. Add the vegetable broth and bring to a boil.
3. Stir in the lentils, dried thyme, bay leaves and parsley.
4. Reduce heat to low and simmer for about 35 minutes.
5. Season with the salt and ground black pepper.

BUTTERNUT
Roast

Prep Time: 30 mins
Total Time: 1 hr 15 mins

Servings per Recipe: 10

Calories	210 kcal
Fat	6 g
Carbohydrates	38.9 g
Protein	3.5 g
Cholesterol	0 mg
Sodium	121 mg

Ingredients

1 butternut squash - peeled, seeded and cut into 1-inch dice
3 carrots, cut into 1 inch pieces
1 large sweet potato, cut into 1-inch cubes
1 rutabaga, peeled and cut into 1-inch pieces

3 parsnips, peeled and cubed
3 turnips, peeled and cut into 1-inch dice
1/4 C. extra virgin olive oil
kosher salt and pepper to taste

Directions

1. Set your oven to 450 degrees F before doing anything else.
2. In a large bowl, add all the
3. Ingredients and toss to coat.
4. Place the vegetable mixture into a deep roasting pan.
5. Cook in the oven for about 45 minutes, stirring once in the middle way.

Comstock
Stew

🥣 Prep Time: 25 mins
🕐 Total Time: 1 hr 25 mins

Servings per Recipe: 75
Calories	108 kcal
Fat	0.8 g
Carbohydrates	24g
Protein	4.2 g
Cholesterol	0 mg
Sodium	196 mg

Ingredients

1 1/2 gallons vegetable broth
4 butternut squashes - peeled, seeded, and diced
6 bunches mustard greens, chopped
7 heads cauliflower, cut into florets
7 heads broccoli, cut into florets
7 red bell peppers, diced
15 carrots, peeled and diced
15 parsnips, diced
1 1/2 onions, diced

1 1/2 stalks celery, diced
3/4 C. raisins
1/4 C. curry powder
1/4 C. ground ginger
1/4 C. ground cumin
1 1/2 tsp cayenne pepper

Directions

1. In a large pan, mix together the vegetable broth, butternut squash, mustard greens, cauliflower, broccoli, red bell peppers, carrots, parsnips, onions, celery, raisins, curry powder, ginger, cumin and cayenne pepper and bring to a boil.

2. Reduce the heat to medium-low and simmer for about 1 hour.

EVERY
Veggie Chips with Dip

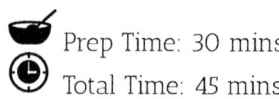

Prep Time: 30 mins
Total Time: 45 mins

Servings per Recipe: 6
Calories	275 kcal
Fat	18.2 g
Carbohydrates	25g
Protein	4.6 g
Cholesterol	8 mg
Sodium	124 mg

Ingredients

1 quart peanut oil for frying, or as needed
1 large beet, peeled and sliced paper-thin
1 large sweet potato, peeled and sliced paper-thin
1 turnip, peeled and sliced paper-thin
1 parsnip, peeled and sliced paper-thin
1 golden beet, peeled and sliced paper-thin
sea salt to taste
freshly cracked black pepper to taste

1 tbsp malt vinegar
1 C. plain Greek yogurt
1/4 C. chopped fresh parsley
1 tbsp chopped fresh mint
1 clove garlic, finely minced
4 green onions, finely chopped
2 tbsp lemon juice
salt and ground white pepper to taste

Directions

1. In a deep-fryer, heat the oil to 360 degrees F.
2. Carefully in batches, fry the beet, sweet potato, turnip, parsnip and golden beet slices for about 2-4 minutes.
3. With a slotted spoon, transfer the vegetable chips onto paper towel plates to drain.
4. Keep aside to cool.
5. Season the chips with the sea salt, cracked black pepper and malt vinegar.
6. In a bowl, mix together the yogurt, parsley, mint, garlic, green onions, lemon juice, salt, and white pepper.

Central European
Lamb Stew

🥣 Prep Time: 15 mins
🕐 Total Time: 2 hrs

Servings per Recipe: 6
Calories	609 kcal
Fat	35.1 g
Carbohydrates	43.4g
Protein	29.8 g
Cholesterol	109 mg
Sodium	325 mg

Ingredients

1 tbsp olive oil
2 lb. boneless lamb shoulder, cut into 1 1/2 inch pieces
1/2 tsp salt
freshly ground black pepper to taste
1 large onion, sliced
2 carrots, peeled and cut into large chunks
1 parsnip, peeled and cut into large chunks (optional)
4 C. water, or as needed

3 large potatoes, peeled and quartered
1 tbsp chopped fresh rosemary (optional)
1 C. coarsely chopped leeks
chopped fresh parsley for garnish (optional)

Directions

1. In a large Dutch oven, heat the oil on medium heat and cook the lamb pieces till browned completely.
2. Season with the salt and pepper.
3. Add the onion, carrots and parsnips and cook for a few minutes.
4. Stir in the water and bring to a boil.
5. Reduce the heat to low.
6. Simmer, covered for about 1 hour.
7. Stir in the potatoes and simmer for about 15-20 minutes.
8. Stir in the leeks and rosemary and simmer, uncovered till potatoes are tender but still whole.
9. Serve with a garnishing of the fresh parsley.

TUESDAY'S
Turkey Thigh Dinner

Prep Time: 25 mins
Total Time: 8 hrs 25 mins

Servings per Recipe: 6

Calories	339 kcal
Fat	6.2 g
Carbohydrates	34.3g
Protein	36.5 g
Cholesterol	127 mg
Sodium	888 mg

Ingredients

2 lb. skinless turkey thighs, cubed
salt and ground black pepper to taste
1 (14.5 oz.) can diced tomatoes with juice
1 (6.5 oz.) jar artichoke hearts, drained
3 parsnips, peeled and cubed
1/2 lb. baby carrots
1 yellow squash, cubed

1 green bell pepper, cut into chunks
4 C. chicken broth
2 cubes chicken bouillon
1 (15 oz.) can garbanzo beans, drained
1 tsp chopped fresh dill

Directions

1. Season the turkey thigh cubes with the salt and black pepper and place into a slow cooker.
2. Pour the diced tomatoes over the turkey, followed by the artichoke hearts, parsnips, baby carrots, yellow squash and green bell pepper.
3. Add the chicken broth to cover.
4. Place the bouillon cubes into the broth.
5. Set the slow cooker on Low and cook, covered for about 8-10 hours.
6. In the last hour of cooking, stir in the garbanzo beans.
7. Serve with a garnishing of the fresh dill.

Alternative
Veggie Cake

🥣 Prep Time: 30 mins
🕐 Total Time: 55 mins

Servings per Recipe: 8
Calories   101 kcal
Fat   0.9 g
Carbohydrates   21.5g
Protein   3.4 g
Cholesterol   23 mg
Sodium   21 mg

Ingredients

3 yellow potatoes, peeled and grated
1 large carrot, peeled and grated
1 parsnip, peeled and grated
1 1/2 C. grated butternut squash
1 egg

1/2 C. whole wheat flour
1 tbsp ground cinnamon

Directions

1. Set your oven to 400 degrees F before doing anything else and grease a baking sheet.
2. In a large bowl, mix together the potatoes, carrot, parsnip and squash.
3. With your hands, squeeze the vegetables in the bowl to separate the juice.
4. Transfer the vegetables into another bowl and mix in the cinnamon.
5. After 5 minutes, slowly pour out the juice from the first bowl.
6. The bottom of the bowl should be coated with the starch.
7. In the bowl of starch, add the egg and flour and with a fork mix to combine.
8. Then take the starch mixture in your hands and massage it through the shredded vegetables.
9. Make about 1-inch thick balls from the mixture and place onto the prepared baking sheet.
10. Flatten the balls to form the patties.
11. Cook in the oven for about 20 minutes.
12. Flip and cook in the oven for about 5 minutes more.

MASHED
Cauliflower and Parsnip

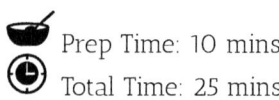

Prep Time: 10 mins
Total Time: 25 mins

Servings per Recipe: 8

Calories	60 kcal
Fat	3.2 g
Carbohydrates	7.3g
Protein	1.9 g
Cholesterol	8 mg
Sodium	95 mg

Ingredients

1 head cauliflower, broken into florets
1 parsnip, peeled and sliced
1/4 C. milk

2 tbsp butter
salt and pepper to taste

Directions

1. Arrange a steamer basket in a pan of water.
2. Cover the pan and bring to a boil.
3. Add the cauliflower and parsnips in steamer basket and steam, covered for about 15 minutes.
4. Drain the vegetables.
5. With a hand masher, mash the vegetables.
6. Slowly, add the milk and butter and mash to desired consistency.
7. Season with the salt and pepper.
8. Serve warm.

American
Spicy Beef Dinner

🥣 Prep Time: 35 mins
🕐 Total Time: 2 hrs 5 mins

Servings per Recipe: 8
Calories	343 kcal
Fat	17.5 g
Carbohydrates	40.7g
Protein	10.3 g
Cholesterol	16 mg
Sodium	159 mg

Ingredients

1/2 lb. beef for stew, such as beef chuck roast, cut into 1-inch chunks
3 tbsp olive oil
2 (3 inch) pieces fresh ginger root, peeled and diced
3 cloves garlic, minced
2 onions, peeled and diced
2 celery ribs, chopped
2 tbsp curry powder
2 tsp coriander powder
1 tsp Asian five-spice powder
1 tsp ground turmeric
2 carrots, peeled and sliced
parsnips, peeled and sliced
2 potatoes, peeled and cubed
1 zucchini, sliced
2 apples - peeled, cored and chopped
1 C. raisins
1 C. cashews
1/2 C. water

Directions

1. Set your oven to 350 degrees F before doing anything else and line a roasting pan with a piece of foil.
2. In a pan, place the beef with enough water to cover and bring to a boil.
3. Reduce the heat and simmer for about 30 minutes.
4. Meanwhile in a deep pan, heat the olive oil on medium-high heat and sauté the ginger, garlic, onions and celery for about 5 minutes.
5. Stir in the curry powder, coriander powder, five-spice powder and turmeric and toss to coat. Cook for about 5 minutes more.
6. Stir in the carrots, parsnips, potatoes, zucchini and apples.
7. Stir in the beef with its cooking liquid, raisins and cashews and toss to coat well.
8. Place the beef and vegetable mixture into the prepared roasting pan.
9. Drizzle 1/2 C. of the water over the mixture and with a piece of foil, cover the pan.
10. Cook in the oven for about 1 hour.

CANADIAN
Country Dinner

Prep Time: 20 mins
Total Time: 50 mins

Servings per Recipe: 6

Calories	288 kcal
Fat	8.2 g
Carbohydrates	54.2g
Protein	4.2 g
Cholesterol	20 mg
Sodium	530 mg

Ingredients

1/4 C. butter, melted
1/4 C. maple syrup
1 tsp salt
1/2 tsp ground black pepper
1 small butternut squash - peeled, seeded, and cubed

2 turnips, cubed
2 parsnips, cut into rounds
1 sweet potato, cubed
1 rutabaga, peeled and cubed
2 carrots, cut into rounds

Directions

1. Set your oven to 350 degrees F before doing anything else and line a roasting pan with a piece of foil.
2. In a large bowl, add the butter, maple syrup, salt and black pepper and beat till well combined.
3. Add the squash, turnips, parsnips, sweet potato, rutabaga and carrots and toss to coat evenly.
4. Place the vegetable mixture into the prepared roasting pan.
5. Cook in the oven for about 30 minutes.

Dublin
Dinner Pie

Prep Time: 45 mins
Total Time: 1 hr 10 mins

Servings per Recipe: 4

Calories	476 kcal
Fat	18.1 g
Carbohydrates	51.4g
Protein	27.5 g
Cholesterol	84 mg
Sodium	1529 mg

Ingredients

1 stalk celery, chopped
3 carrots, peeled and chopped
1 parsnip, peeled and diced
1 small rutabaga, chopped
1/4 C. frozen green peas
1 lb. ground lamb
1 onion, chopped
1 clove garlic, chopped
1 (8 oz.) can tomato sauce

1 tsp salt
1/2 tsp ground black pepper
1/4 tsp dried thyme
1/4 tsp dried sage
1/2 C. milk
3 C. prepared mashed potatoes
2 tbsp grated Parmesan cheese

Directions

1. Set your oven to 350 degrees F before doing anything else and grease a 7x11-inch baking dish.
2. In a large pan, place the celery, carrots, parsnip, rutabaga, peas and 1-inch of water and bring to a boil.
3. Cook, covered for about 15 minutes.
4. Meanwhile, heat a large skillet on medium heat and crumble in the ground lamb.
5. Add the onion and garlic and cook till the lamb is no longer pink.
6. Drain off any grease.
7. Stir in the steamed vegetables, tomato sauce, salt, pepper, thyme and sage.
8. Transfer the lamb mixture into prepared baking dish.
9. Add enough milk into the mashed potatoes and mix well.
10. Spread the potato mixture over the lamb mixture and sprinkle with the Parmesan cheese.
11. Cook in the oven for about 25 minutes.

CHICKEN
Barley Soup 101

Prep Time: 20 mins
Total Time: 1 hr 30 mins

Servings per Recipe: 16

Calories	240 kcal
Fat	3.5 g
Carbohydrates	41.3g
Protein	11.8 g
Cholesterol	20 mg
Sodium	530 mg

Ingredients

2 tsp olive oil
1 Spanish onion, diced
1/2 C. diced celery
3 cloves garlic, minced
2 1/2 quarts chicken stock
3 C. diced cooked chicken breast
3 C. sliced carrots

2 parsnips, diced (optional)
1 1/4 C. barley
4 large sweet potatoes, peeled and diced
1/2 C. chopped fresh dill (optional)
salt and ground black pepper to taste

Directions

1. In a large heavy stock pan, heat the olive oil on medium heat and sauté the onion, celery and garlic for about 8 minutes.
2. Stir in the chicken stock, chicken, carrots, parsnips and barley and bring to a boil.
3. Reduce the heat and simmer for about 30 minutes.
4. Stir in the sweet potatoes and simmer for about 30 minutes.
5. Season with the dill, salt and pepper.

Greek Style
Veggie Patties

Prep Time: 15 mins
Total Time: 45 mins

Servings per Recipe: 6
Calories	223 kcal
Fat	15.8 g
Carbohydrates	15.4g
Protein	7.1 g
Cholesterol	69 mg
Sodium	446 mg

Ingredients

1/4 C. olive oil, divided
1 C. finely chopped onion
3 cloves garlic, chopped
3 C. roughly chopped spinach
1 large parsnip, grated
1/3 C. chopped artichoke hearts
1/3 C. chopped Kalamata olives
1/3 C. almond flour
1/4 C. finely chopped sun-dried tomatoes

3 small eggs, beaten
2 tbsp finely chopped walnuts
1/2 tsp salt
1/4 tsp ground black pepper

Directions

1. In a skillet, heat 2 tbsp of the olive oil on medium heat and sauté the onion and garlic for about 5 minutes.
2. Add the spinach and cook for about 5 minutes.
3. Transfer the spinach mixture into a large bowl and keep aside to cool for about 5-10 minutes.
4. In the bowl of spinach mixture, add the parsnip, artichoke hearts, olives, almond flour, tomatoes, eggs, walnuts, salt and pepper and mix till well combined.
5. Make 6 equal sized cakes from the mixture.
6. In a skillet, heat the remaining 2 tbsp of the olive oil and cook the cakes for about 5 minutes per side.

BAKED
Veggie Hodgepodge

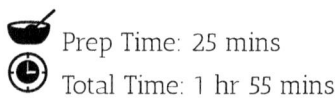

Prep Time: 25 mins
Total Time: 1 hr 55 mins

Servings per Recipe: 6

Calories	191 kcal
Fat	5 g
Carbohydrates	34.6g
Protein	4 g
Cholesterol	0 mg
Sodium	257 mg

Ingredients

2 tbsp olive oil, divided
1 large yam, peeled and cut into 1 inch pieces
1 large parsnip, peeled and cut into 1 inch pieces
1 C. baby carrots
1 zucchini, cut into 1 inch slices
1 bunch fresh asparagus, trimmed and cut into 1 inch pieces
1/2 C. roasted red peppers, cut into 1-inch pieces
2 cloves garlic, minced
1/4 C. chopped fresh basil
1/2 tsp kosher salt
1/2 tsp ground black pepper

Directions

1. Set your oven to 425 degrees F before doing anything else and grease 2 baking sheets.
2. Arrange the yams, parsnips and carrots onto the baking sheets.
3. Cook in the oven for about 30 minutes.
4. Now in the baking sheets, add the zucchini and asparagus and drizzle with the remaining 1 tbsp of the olive oil.
5. Cook in the oven for about 30 minutes more.
6. Remove from the oven and keep aside to cool for about 30 minutes.
7. In a large bowl, add the roasted peppers, garlic, basil, salt and pepper and toss to coat.
8. Add the roasted vegetables and toss to mix.
9. Serve at room temperature or cold.

Hot
Veggie Gumbo

🍲 Prep Time: 45 mins

🕐 Total Time: 2 hrs

Servings per Recipe: 8

Calories	268 kcal
Fat	11.8 g
Carbohydrates	35.7g
Protein	6.8 g
Cholesterol	0 mg
Sodium	886 mg

Ingredients

1 serrano pepper
1 banana pepper
1 small jalapeno chili pepper
1/4 C. canola oil
1/4 C. all-purpose flour
2 tbsp canola oil
2 celery ribs, chopped
1 large onion, chopped
3 green bell peppers, chopped
1 quart vegetable broth
2 cloves garlic, minced
2 tbsp Cajun seasoning

1 tbsp smoked paprika
1 tbsp file powder
1 C. fire-roasted tomatoes
1 sweet potato, peeled and cubed
parsnip, peeled and cubed
1 C. canned red beans, rinsed and drained
1 C. canned black-eyed peas, rinsed and drained
2 C. frozen cut okra, thawed

Directions

1. In a baking sheet, arrange the Serrano, banana, and jalapeño chili peppers.
2. Cook under the broiler for about 4-5 minutes.
3. Turn the peppers and cook under the broiler till blackened from all sides.
4. Remove the peppers from the oven and place in a sealed paper bag to steam for about 15 to 20 minutes.
5. Remove the peppers from the bag and peel off the crispy black skin.
6. Remove the stems and seeds from the peppers and chop roughly.
7. Place the peppers in a bowl.
8. In a large skillet, heat the canola oil on medium heat and slowly, add the flour, beating continuously.
9. Cook for about 20 minutes, beating continuously.
10. Remove the roux from the heat.

11. In a deep soup pan, heat 2 tbsp of the canola oil on medium-high heat and sauté the celery, half of the onions and bell peppers for about 5 minutes.
12. Stir in 1/4 C. of the vegetable broth and simmer, covered for about 10-15 minutes.
13. Stir the serrano, banana, and jalapeño chili peppers, uncooked bell peppers, onions, garlic, Cajun seasoning, smoked paprika and file powder.
14. Add the roux and 1 C. of the stock, stirring continuously till the roux dissolves.
15. Simmer, covered for about 5 minutes.
16. Add the tomatoes, sweet potato, parsnip, red beans, black-eyed peas, okra and remaining stock and simmer, uncovered for about 30 minutes.
17. Season to taste with salt and pepper.

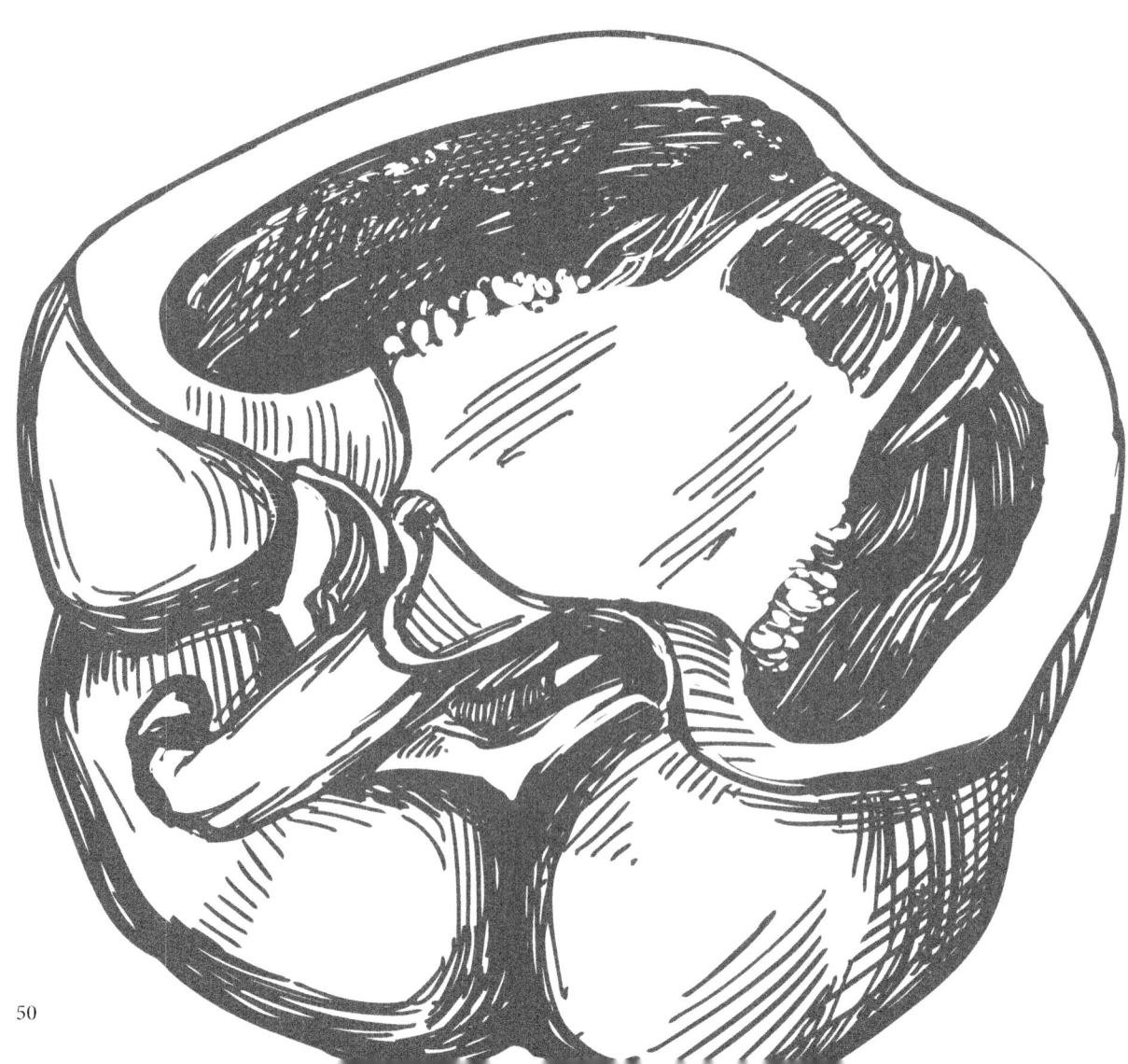

Chicken
and Parsnip Combination Platter

Prep Time: 15 mins
Total Time: 1 hr

Servings per Recipe: 4

Calories	414 kcal
Fat	13.9 g
Carbohydrates	43.4g
Protein	28.2 g
Cholesterol	68 mg
Sodium	586 mg

Ingredients

Vegetables:
3 C. peeled and cubed butternut squash
2 carrots, peeled and cut 1-inch pieces
1 large parsnip, peeled and cut into 1/2-inch pieces
1 small sweet potato, peeled and cut into 1/2-inch pieces
1 small red onion, cut into 1-inch wedges
2 tbsp extra-virgin olive oil
2 tsp minced fresh rosemary
1/2 tsp sea salt
1/4 tsp fresh ground black pepper

Chicken:
4 skinless, boneless chicken breast halves
1/4 tsp salt
1 pinch ground black pepper to taste
1 tbsp extra-virgin olive oil
1/2 C. low-sodium chicken broth
1/4 C. water
2 tbsp honey
2 tbsp whole-grain mustard

Directions

1. Set your oven to 425 degrees F before doing anything else.
2. Arrange an 11x17-inch baking sheet in the oven while heating.
3. In a large bowl, add the butternut squash, carrots, parsnip, sweet potato, red onion, and 2 tbsp of the olive oil, rosemary, 1/2 tsp of the sea salt and 1/4 tsp of the pepper and toss to coat.
4. In the warmed baking sheet, spread the vegetable mixture in a single layer
5. Cook in the oven for about 15 minutes.
6. Remove from the oven and stir the vegetable mixture.
7. Cook in the oven for about 15 minutes more.
8. Place the chicken onto a work surface and pound into 1/2-inch thickness.
9. Season the chicken with 1/4 tsp of the salt and ground black pepper.
10. In a large skillet, heat 1 tbsp of the olive oil on medium heat and cook the chicken for

about 5 minutes per side.

11. Transfer the chicken into a bowl.
12. In the same skillet, add the chicken broth and water and bring to a boil, scraping the browned bits from the bottom of the pan with a wooden spoon for about 2 minutes.
13. Stir in the honey, mustard and chicken.
14. Serve chicken alongside the roasted vegetables.

Granny Smith Dessert

🥣 Prep Time: 10 mins
🕐 Total Time: 20 mins

Servings per Recipe: 4
Calories	112 kcal
Fat	3.1 g
Carbohydrates	22.3g
Protein	0.9 g
Cholesterol	8 mg
Sodium	28 mg

Ingredients

1 tbsp butter
2 Granny Smith apples, peeled and diced
1 large parsnip, peeled and cut into long thin pieces
2 tbsp water

1 tbsp brown sugar
1/2 tsp ground cinnamon

Directions

1. In a pan, melt the butter and cook the apples and parsnip for about 5 minutes.
2. Stir in the water, brown sugar and cinnamon and cook for about 5 minutes.
3. Serve warm or cold.

OCTOBER'S
Pancakes

Prep Time: 15 mins
Total Time: 25 mins

Servings per Recipe: 4
Calories   200 kcal
Fat   6.4 g
Carbohydrates   28.8g
Protein   7.2 g
Cholesterol   104 mg
Sodium   114 mg

Ingredients

1 C. shredded parsnip
1 C. shredded carrot
1 scallion, chopped
3/4 C. all-purpose flour
1 pinch salt and ground black pepper to
taste

1/2 C. half-and-half
2 eggs

Directions

1. In a bowl, add the parsnip, carrot, scallion, flour, salt and pepper and toss to coat.
2. In another bowl, add the half-and-half and eggs and beat till smooth.
3. Slowly, place the egg mixture over the parsnip mixture, stirring continuously.
4. Make equal sized patties from the mixture.
5. Heat a large skillet on medium-high heat and place the patties in it.
6. With the back of a spatula, flatten the patties and cook for about 5 minutes per side.

How to Make
Parsnip Gratin

🥣 Prep Time: 15 mins
🕐 Total Time: 2 hrs 11 mins

Servings per Recipe: 4
Calories	935 kcal
Fat	71.8 g
Carbohydrates	50g
Protein	27.1 g
Cholesterol	234 mg
Sodium	1175 mg

Ingredients

1/4 C. butter
2 lb. parsnips
1 C. freshly grated Parmigiano-Reggiano cheese
2 ribs celery, chopped
2 leeks, chopped and divided
3 cloves garlic, crushed and divided
2 slices fresh ginger root
sea salt and freshly ground black pepper to taste

1/2 tsp ground cloves
3 C. water
2 bay leaves
2 sprigs fresh rosemary leaves, divided
1 (3 oz.) piece of Parmigiano-Reggiano rind
2 C. heavy whipping cream

Directions

1. Set your oven to 375 degrees F before doing anything else and grease a 2-quart baking dish.
2. Peel the parsnips, reserving peelings for broth.
3. Cut the parsnips into 1/8-inch rounds.
4. In the prepared baking dish, arrange 1/3 of the parsnip slices in a single layer and sprinkle with 1/3 of the Parmigiano cheese.
5. Repeat with the remaining parsnips and Parmigiano cheese.
6. In a large skillet, melt 1 tbsp of the butter on medium heat and cook the celery, 1/2 of the leeks, 1 garlic clove and ginger pieces for about 5 minutes.
7. Add the parsnip peelings, salt, pepper, cloves and 2 tbsp of the water and cook for about 5 minutes, stirring continuously.
8. Cook, adding water as needed for about 8-10 minutes, stirring continuously.
9. Add remaining water, bay leaves, 1 sprig of the rosemary and Parmigiano rind and increase the heat to high.

10. Bring to a boil.
11. Reduce the heat and simmer, covered for about 20-30 minutes.
12. Season with the salt, pepper and cloves and remove from heat.
13. Through a fine sieve, strain the broth pressing solids to extract as much liquid as possible.
14. In a pan, melt the remaining butter on medium heat and cook the remaining leeks, remaining garlic and several rosemary leaves for about 5 minutes.
15. Add the reserved broth and cook for about 10-12 minutes.
16. Stir in the cream, salt, pepper and cloves and cook for about 3 minutes.
17. Transfer the mixture into the prepared baking dish to 3/4 of the way up parsnip layers.
18. Cook in the oven for about 45-60 minutes.
19. Remove from the oven and keep aside to cool for about 10 minutes.
20. Serve with a garnishing of the cloves and rosemary leaves.

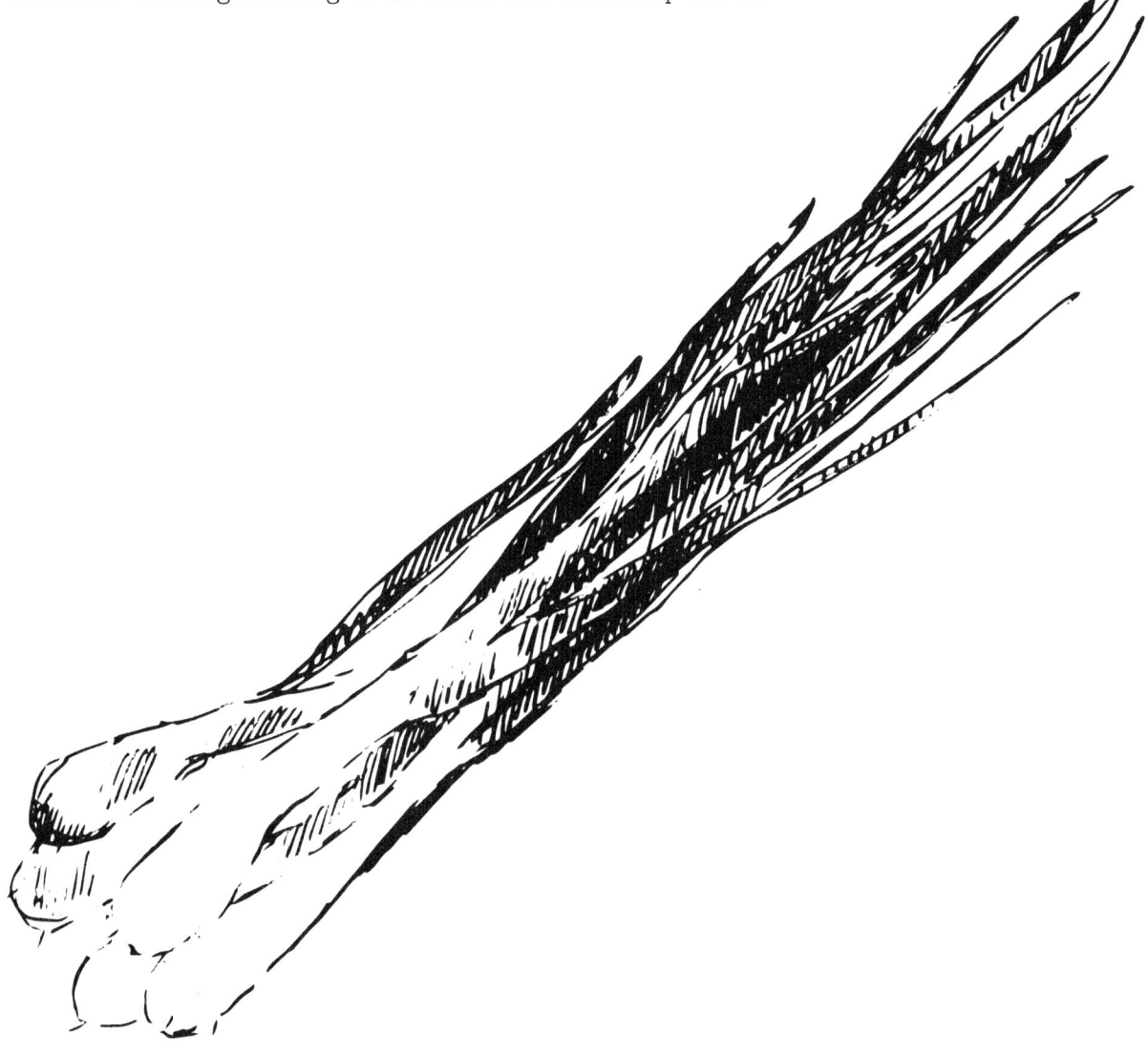

Root Vegetables
with Seoul (Korean Inspired)

Prep Time: 30 mins
Total Time: 2 hrs

Servings per Recipe: 6
Calories	192 kcal
Fat	14.1 g
Carbohydrates	13.5g
Protein	4.2 g
Cholesterol	7 mg
Sodium	880 mg

Ingredients

1 Korean radish, peeled and cut into 1/2-inch squares
2 turnips, peeled and cut into 1/4-inch squares
1 large parsnip, peeled and cut into 1-inch pieces
2 large cloves garlic, thinly sliced
1/4 C. soy sauce
1/4 C. sesame oil
1 tbsp olive oil

1 tsp freshly ground black pepper
1/4 tsp salt
1/8 tsp red pepper flakes
4 slices turkey bacon, sliced into 1/4-inch strips
2 2-inch fresh thyme sprigs

Directions

1. Set your oven to 420 degrees F before doing anything else.
2. In a gallon-size resealable plastic bag, place the radish, turnips, parsnip pieces, garlic, soy sauce, sesame oil, olive oil, and black pepper, salt, and red pepper flakes.
3. Seal the bag and shake to coat well.
4. Keep aside to marinate for about 10 minutes.
5. Shake the bag over and marinate for about 10 minutes more.
6. Transfer the marinated vegetables into a 1 1/2-inch deep baking dish into an even layer.
7. Top with the bacon and thyme evenly.
8. Cook in the oven for about 55 minutes
9. Remove from the oven and stir the vegetables.
10. Cook in the oven for about 15 minutes more.

4-INGREDIENT
Parsnip Fries

Prep Time: 5 mins
Total Time: 45 mins

Servings per Recipe: 6
Calories	166.8
Fat	5.1g
Cholesterol	0.0mg
Sodium	17.5mg
Carbohydrates	30.2g
Protein	2.1g

Ingredients

2 lbs parsnip, peeled and halved length ways
2 tbsp olive oil

1 1/4 tsp ground cumin
3 tsp fresh thyme

Directions

1. Set your oven to 400 degrees F before doing anything else.
2. In a bowl, add the parsnips, olive oil and cumin and toss to coat.
3. Transfer the mixture into a baking dish.
4. Cook in the oven for about 30 - 40 minutes.

Printed in Great Britain
by Amazon

77900086R00034